SPOTLIGHT ON PHYSICAL SCIENCE

MIXTURES AND SOLUTIONS

IT MATTERS

BARBARA M. LINDE

PowerKiDS press™

NEW YORK

Acknowledgments: Jeffrey A. Hinkley, Ph.D., Chemistry, subject matter expert

Published in 2020 by The Rosen Publishing Group, Inc.
29 East 21st Street, New York, NY 10010

Editor: Jennifer Lombardo
Book Design: Michael Flynn

Photo Credits: Cover, p. 1 SUWIT NGAOKAEW/Shutterstock.com; (series molecular background) pro500/Shutterstock.com; p. 4 Africa Studio/Shutterstock.com; p. 5 Elena Veselova/Shutterstock.com; pp. 6, 12 Syda Productions/Shutterstock.com; p. 7 alexandre zveiger/Shutterstock.com; p. 9 (cookies) Alexeysun/Shutterstock.com; p. 9 (coffee) SJ Travel Photo and Video/Shutterstock.com; p. 11 Leemage/Universal Images Group/Getty Images; p. 13 Olga Miltsova/Shutterstock.com; p. 15 RossHelen/Shutterstock.com; p. 16 https://en.wikipedia.org/wiki/Norbert_Rillieux#/media/File:NorbertRillieux.jpg; p. 17 Hywit Dimyadi/Shutterstock.com; p. 18 lightpoet/Shutterstock.com; p. 19 WLADIMIR BULGAR/Science Photo Library/Getty Images; p. 21 Chris Ware/Hulton Archive/Getty Images; p. 22 CL Shebley/Shutterstock.com; p. 23 Thongsuk Atiwannakul/Shutterstock.com; p. 24 franz12/Shutterstock.com; p. 25 worker/Shutterstock.com; p. 26 Designua/Shutterstock.com; p. 27 ETAJOE/Shutterstock.com; p. 28 MO_SES Premium/Shutterstock.com; p. 29 noPPonPat/Shutterstock.com; p. 30 Monkey Business Images/Shutterstock.com.

Library of Congress Cataloging-in-Publication Data

Names: Linde, Barbara M.
Title: Mixtures and solutions: it matters / Barbara M. Linde.
Description: New York : PowerKids Press, 2020. | Series: Spotlight on physical science | Includes glossary and index.
Identifiers: ISBN 9781725313248 (pbk.) | ISBN 9781725313279 (library bound) | ISBN 9781725313255 (6 pack)
Subjects: LCSH: Solution (Chemistry)--Juvenile literature. | Mixtures--Juvenile literature. | Chemistry--Juvenile literature.
Classification: LCC QD541.R43 2020 | DDC 541'.34--dc23

Manufactured in the United States of America

CPSIA Compliance Information: Batch #CWPK20. For further information contact Rosen Publishing, New York, New York at 1-800-237-9932.

CONTENTS

CHAPTER ONE

IT'S A MIXTURE

What do you get when you mix two or more things together? Most of the time, you get a mixture. A mixture of sand and water makes wet sand. A mixture of candy, fruit, and nuts is trail mix. You haven't created any new materials. The things in a mixture can be separated again. You can let the sand dry out. You can pick the nuts out of the trail mix. Sometimes it's easy to separate the parts. Other times, it's much harder. You might need special tools.

The parts of a mixture can be solids, liquids, or gases. Toothpaste is a mixture. Often, two of its parts are a solid powder and liquid water. Smoke is a mixture of bits of solid **soot** combined with air and other things. Fog is a mixture of water droplets and air.

It's easy to tell that this trail mix is a mixture because you can see each separate part of it.

CHAPTER TWO

IT'S A SOLUTION

A solution is a special kind of mixture. You can't see the parts that make it up. When you mix a little sugar with water, they make a solution because the sugar **dissolves**. The sugar and water are still there, but they mix so well that you can't see the sugar. The water is the solvent and the sugar is the solute. If you let the solution **evaporate**, the liquid water will disappear and the sugar will be **visible** again.

You can't see the chlorine gas in a swimming pool because it has dissolved.

Like other mixtures, solutions can be made of solids, liquids, and gases. The water in a swimming pool is a solution because it has **chlorine** gas dissolved in it. You can **dilute** a solution by adding more solvent. You can concentrate it, or make it stronger, by taking solvent away or adding more solute.

CHAPTER THREE

HOMOGENEOUS AND HETEROGENEOUS

A mixture is heterogeneous if it isn't the same everywhere. A chocolate chip cookie is a heterogeneous mixture of chocolate chips and cookie dough. The cookie is heterogeneous because you can see where the chips are and where there's just cookie dough. There's usually more cookie dough than chips.

A mixture is homogeneous if every part of it looks the same. A homogeneous mixture isn't a solution because nothing is dissolved. However, a homogeneous mixture can be made from solutions. For example, lemonade is a solution of sugar in lemon juice and water, and sweet iced tea is a solution of sugar in tea. Mixing iced tea with lemonade creates a homogenous mixture. The iced tea and lemonade aren't dissolving in each other, but they're mixing so well that you can't see which parts are lemonade and which are iced tea.

In heterogeneous mixtures, it's easy to see all the separate parts. Sometimes homogeneous mixtures become heterogeneous if they sit long enough; the parts separate on their own and become easy to see.

CHAPTER FOUR

METAL MIXTURES IN HISTORY

For many years, copper was the only known metal. People found the pure metal in the ground and used it for things such as tools and jewelry. Around 3000 BC, people figured out how to get tin from rocks and then discovered tin and copper could be melted together. They make a solution called bronze. Bronze is stronger than copper, and it makes strong tools and armor. The change from stone to bronze tools was a big event that changed the way people live. We call the time immediately after that the Bronze Age.

A solution of two or more metals (or a metal and a nonmetal) is also called an alloy. Copper can make other alloys besides bronze. One of them is brass, an alloy of copper and zinc. The use of brass started spreading about 100 BC. The Romans used it for coins.

This bronze armor was made in Greece around 600 BC.

CHAPTER FIVE

NOT A CHEMICAL REACTION

Making a mixture is different from causing a chemical reaction because a chemical reaction changes a substance in a way that can't be easily undone. The substances involved in a chemical reaction can't be separated again. For example, a car uses heat to burn gasoline to release energy to make the car move. Without heat, the gasoline and the car engine are just a mixture. You can take the gasoline back out of the car. Once the heat is added, though, the gasoline is changed and you can't get it back.

A toasted marshmallow is the result of a chemical reaction, but a s'more is a mixture.

Another way you can tell the difference between a reaction and a mixture is that chemical reactions give off energy, often in the form of light or heat, but mixtures don't. You can't use trail mix to power a car or use a bronze bracelet to light your way in the dark.

CHAPTER SIX

MAKING MIXTURES

Some mixtures are easy to make; we do it every day, often without even thinking about it. However, others take a lot of work to get right. Paint is an example of a tricky mixture. Every paint is made up of three main parts. The color comes from a solid **pigment**. A binder is a substance that holds the mixture together. A solvent thins the mixture to make it easier to apply.

If you go to a paint store, you'll find many cans of paint. There are two main kinds of paint mixtures. In a water-based paint, the solvent is water. In an oil-based paint, the solvent is oil. If you add water to oil-based paint, the water won't dissolve. The oil and water layers will separate, and you won't be able to use the paint.

To make sure everything is mixed right, paint companies and hardware stores use a machine that shakes the paint much faster than a person could stir it.

CHAPTER SEVEN

SEPARATING MIXTURES

Some mixtures separate on their own, but sometimes it takes work to separate them. For example, in the early 1900s, a man named Norbert Rillieux thought of a new way to produce sugar from a plant called sugarcane. The first step in making sugar is to crush the sugarcane. This makes a juice that contains both sugar and water. To make pure sugar, people need to remove the water. In the 1800s, workers did this by boiling the juice in a series of large pots over wood fires. The process was unsafe and expensive. It used a lot of wood and ruined some of the sugar by burning it.

NORBERT RILLIEUX

Norbert Rillieux, one of the first chemical engineers in the United States, came up with the idea of using boilers to evaporate the water to produce sugar. Today, the boilers are bigger, but the process is mostly the same.

Rillieux made a new process that used closed boilers to evaporate the water. His sugar tasted better and didn't burn. The process cost less and was safer. It quickly spread around the world, and we still use it today.

CHAPTER EIGHT

CHROMATOGRAPHY

One way to separate a mixture is called chromatography. The first step in chromatography is to combine the mixture with a liquid or gas, which is called the mobile phase. The mobile phase is then poured into or onto a solid or liquid substance called the stationary phase. You need a different stationary phase for different kinds of mixtures. The different parts of the mixture move through the stationary phase at different speeds, allowing scientists to collect one part at a time.

This scientist is examining a chromatogram. Mixtures started out as strips at the bottom. Parts of the mixtures moved up to make separate spots.

One kind of chromatography uses a special piece of paper. A tiny drop or thin stripe of the mixture is placed near the bottom of the paper with a liquid solvent. The solvent soaks into and travels along the paper. The parts of the mixture that dissolved move with the solvent. Other parts may not dissolve and don't move.

CHAPTER NINE

FUEL

In some places, a mixture known as petroleum formed underground when dead plants and animals were buried and subjected to extreme heat and pressure over many years. In 1853, a man named Abraham Gesner discovered how to separate parts of that mixture. Using a process called **distillation**, he removed a liquid called kerosene from petroleum. Kerosene lamps produced more light than candles and gave off less smoke than whale oil lamps. Hospitals started using kerosene. Soon after, it started to be used in streetlights, too. Over time, scientists also learned how to create a mixture called gasoline from petroleum. This is what we use to power our cars and planes.

In 1854, Gesner helped set up a factory to make kerosene. Most people don't use this substance anymore, but his work led to the creation of today's oil **industry**.

Until the late 1800s, someone had to light streetlights by hand at night and put them out in the morning.

CHAPTER TEN

SOLAR CELLS

Solar cells can create electricity when the sun shines on them. Most solar cells are made of **silicon** mixtures. The silicon has to be very pure. Only 10 atoms out of 1 million can be something other than silicon. After that, engineers mix in tiny amounts of other atoms. A solar cell has two layers. Each layer is a different mixture. The two layers turn sunlight into electricity.

A scientist used silicon mixtures to make the first solar cells in 1954. Over time, other scientists have improved these mixtures. Today's solar cells are six times better than that first one. Only 2 percent of the electricity in the United States comes from solar cells, but that number is growing. Some people add solar panels to their roofs. The panels help power their home.

Large solar panels use solar cells to gather energy from sunlight. The solar cells are made from melted silicon.

CHAPTER ELEVEN

RECYCLING

In most cities, trash is picked up from homes. Too much trash is a problem. In 1980, the first cities began to use curbside recycling. People wanted to reuse some materials instead of adding to landfills. Recyclable materials are those that can be reused. To keep the recyclables separate from the trash, people often use a separate bin. Glass, plastics, and **aluminum** cans are often recycled. So are lots of paper and cardboard.

This is mixed waste at a recycling plant. Heavier items fall through the rotating screen at the top. The rest will be separated again later.

In many places, people create a heterogeneous mixture with their recycling by throwing it all into one bin. When this mixture arrives at the recycling plant, it has to be separated into its separate parts. Some separating is done by hand. Machines also do some sorting. Then the different substances are combined into something new. A box made out of recycled cardboard is a homogeneous mixture made up of what were once separate pieces of cardboard!

CHAPTER TWELVE

REMOVING SALT FROM WATER

About 97 percent of the water on Earth's surface is a solution of salt in water. Every quart (0.95 L) of seawater has about 6 teaspoons of salt. Salt water harms crops, and drinking it makes people sick.

Most living things need water without salt. Taking fresh water out of seawater is a process called desalination. There are a few different ways to do this. You can boil the water and collect the steam. The steam turns back into water, but the salt stays behind in the boiler. Another way is to push the water through a **filter**. Only water can go through. The salt is blocked by the filter. This process is called reverse osmosis.

REVERSE OSMOSIS

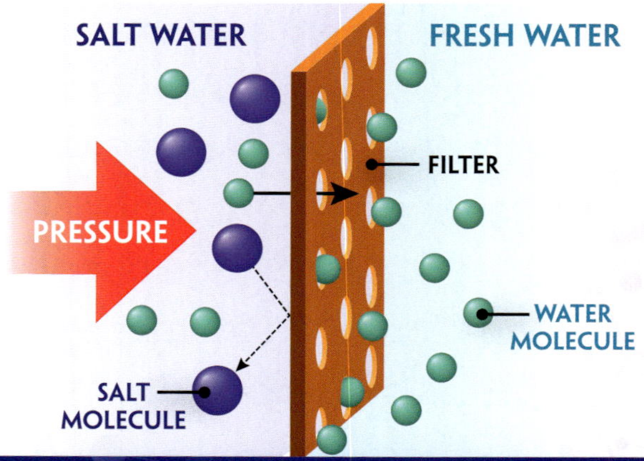

At a reverse osmosis plant, the salt water goes through the white tubes under pressure. Fresh water is filtered into smaller tubes inside.

CHAPTER THIRTEEN

COMPOSITES

The heavier a car is, the more energy it takes to make it move and the more gasoline it uses. To make cars lighter, engineers use plastic to build their frame. Plastic is light, but it's soft and bends easily. To make it stiffer, engineers mix the plastic with glass fibers. Glass is stronger than plastic. It is not as strong as steel or aluminum, but it's much lighter. This mixture is called a composite. A composite is a homogeneous mixture of two or more materials that are very different from each other and make up something completely new—and stronger—when they're combined.

Airplanes also use composites to save weight. For an airplane frame, plastic is mixed with a composite called carbon fiber. Carbon fiber composites are lighter than aluminum but just as strong.

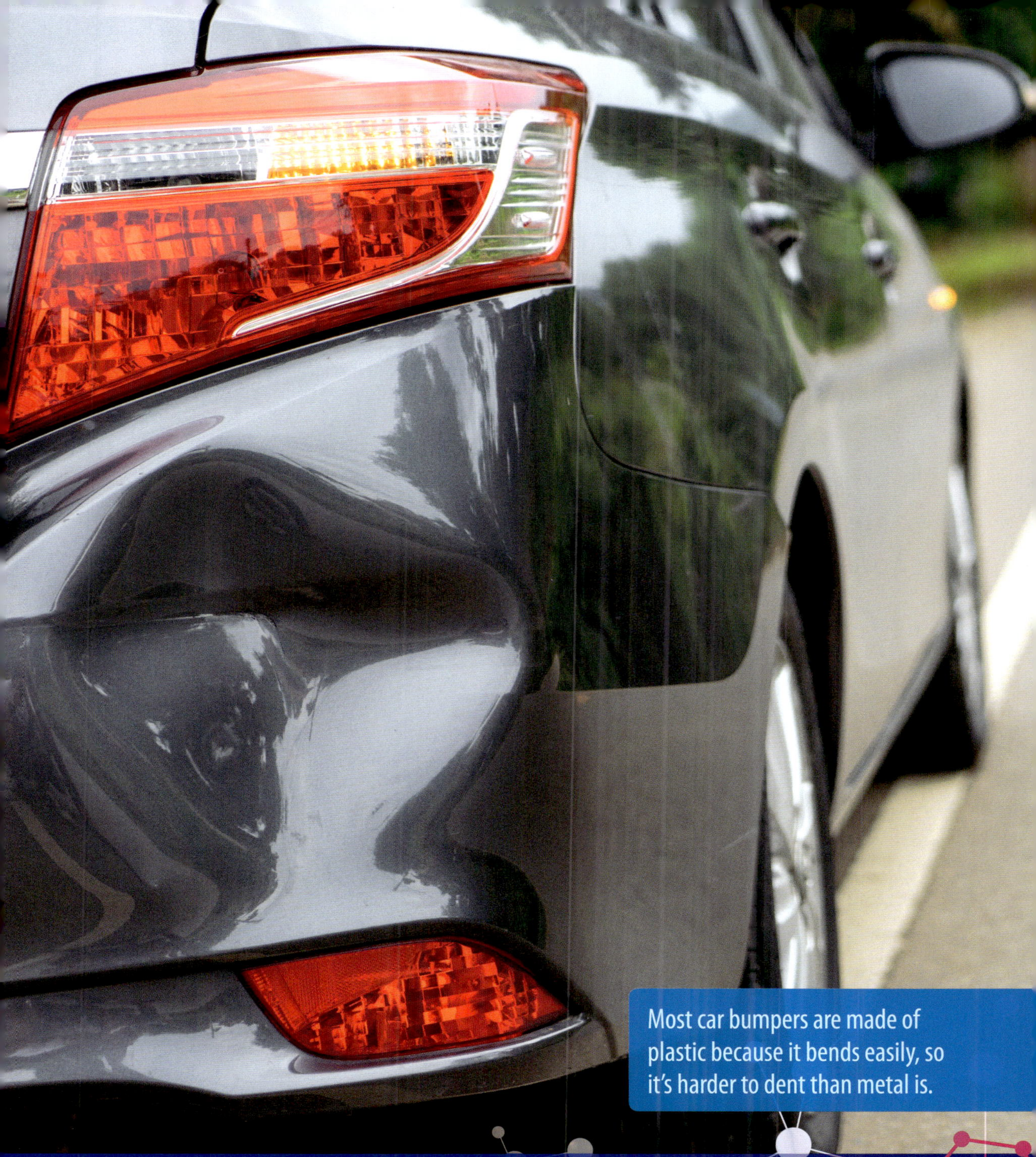

Most car bumpers are made of plastic because it bends easily, so it's harder to dent than metal is.

CHAPTER FOURTEEN

MIXTURES AND SOLUTIONS EVERYWHERE

Now that you know about mixtures and solutions, think like a scientist. Think about the foods you eat. Do you like hot chocolate? That's a solution—and if you add marshmallows, it's a mixture, too! Did you have cereal for breakfast? That's a heterogeneous mixture. The tip of the pencil you use at school is made of a material called graphite, mixed with clay to hold it together. When you help wash the dishes after dinner, you use a solution of water and dish soap. Look out the window of a car or a bus. The road may be a composite of **asphalt** and stone.

Walk around your house. Make a list of the mixtures and solutions you find. Ask your family members to help you. Mixtures and solutions are all around you. To find them, take a careful look.

GLOSSARY

aluminum (uh-LOO-muh-nuhm) A type of lightweight metal.

asphalt (AZ-fawlt) A natural material often used to make roads.

chlorine (kloor-EEN) A chemical element sometimes used to disinfect.

dilute (dye-LOOT) To make thinner by adding more liquid.

dissolve (dih-SOLV) To break down a solid when a liquid mixes with that solid.

distillation (dih-stih-LAY-shun) The process of heating a liquid until it gives off a gas and then cooling the gas until it becomes a liquid.

evaporate (ih-VAA-puh-rayt) To change from a liquid to a gas.

filter (FIL-tuhr) To collect bits from a liquid passing through, or what the liquid passes through.

industry (IN-duhs-tree) A group of businesses that provide a particular product or service.

pigment (PIHG-muhnt) A substance that gives color to something else.

silicon (SIH-lih-kuhn) An element that's often used in computers and electronics.

soot (SOOT) A black powder made from burning wood or coal.

visible (VIH-suh-buhl) Able to be seen.

INDEX

PRIMARY SOURCE LIST

Page 11
Bronze cuirass. c. fourth century BC. Greece.

Page 16
Norbert Rillieux. Photograph. c. 1850s. Photographer unknown.

Page 21
John Jennings, London's oldest lamplighter. Photograph. 1952. Taken in Clerkenwell, London, England.

WEBSITES

Due to the changing nature of Internet links, PowerKids Press has developed an online list of websites related to the subject of this book. This site is updated regularly. Please use this link to access the list: www.powerkidslinks.com/SOPS/mixsolutions